For Mj

On the occasion of the chaotic 2020 election. However this goes, remember — DON'T GIVE IN TO HATE. THAT LEADS TO THE DARK SIDE.

Love,

[signature]

4 November 2020

# Broadcast / Domino / Plague

Poems by Hart L'Ecuyer

Spartan
Press
Kansas City          Missouri

Spartan Press
Kansas City, Missouri
spartanpresskc.com

Spartan
Press

The author would like to acknowledge the extraordinary support of numerous family members (especially Uncle Vince and Uncle John) and friends (especially Tom, Ben and Michael) amid the many trials without which this book would not exist. Further acknowledgment is made to Dr. Ryan Jackson, Dr. Michael Chicoine, and Dr. Hiram Gay and their respective staff, whose world-class surgical and oncological expertise saved the author's life.

# TABLE OF CONTENTS

This one's for the boys.

*America when will you be angelic?*
*When will you take off your clothes?*

-Allen Ginsberg

## SHE TOOK OFF HER CLOTHES

She took off her
clothes in a cornfield. A scarecrow
gave her the side-eye. No men
were with her. There were no women with her.
The austere blue sky was her father's house.

She
took off her clothes at the laundromat.
There was a certain logic to it.

She took off her clothes in the park. A baseball
landed in the grass at her feet; she
collects them.

She took off
her clothes on the overpass.
The red sun sank into the skyline.
The moon was my love for her now.

## MONUMENT GIRLS

the monument fails to recognize the pinup girl she
likens the monument to a penis which is fair her cheeks
look a little thin she sits in the grass to do her nails & feeling
like Jesus I walk straight past not even a glance down
her shirt her shirt is blue & green hey you
know what I change my mind I pick up a rock & throw it at
her because she's so pretty it's unfair for there to be people that
pretty she did not react in a friendly way I guess I should
have expected that she yells at me What The Fuck Dude & so I
run away very fast but I trip on a second pinup girl who is even
prettier than the first one so I throw Two rocks at her now
they are Both chasing me I go into the reflecting pool thinking
they are Witches & witches don't like water but
they are not witches after all so they get in the
pool too it's a shallow ornamental pool black marble they look
so pretty I splash them to lighten the mood but it does not help
they just get madder & madder now more pinup girls are
appearing & they all seem to know exactly what's going on I
try apologizing that doesn't work so maybe more rocks I throw
more rocks but soon I run out of rocks there are thousands of
pinup girls & only nine rocks so I throw the nine rocks at the
nine closest pinup girls & run into the museum which is

Terrifying absolutely terrifying gunfire everywhere
soldiers yelling historical artifacts glowing with radiation evil
museum employees glaring as if I am going to steal the
radioactive boots & radioactive radios & radioactive bullets
it was all very upsetting

## HAIR SALON GIRLS

what's behind the curtains I wonder so I get real
close to the curtains & try to open them but the
curtains turn out to be some girl's sweater & I explained
see I thought your sweater was curtains easy
mistake to make she said Go Away so I entered a
coffeeshop but it was unlike any coffeeshop I had seen
before instead of coffee they had hair dryers & instead of
steam wands they had scissors & instead of cups they
had wash basins they asked if I wanted a haircut I said no I
want a cup of coffee they said we don't have any I said well
pretty lousy of you given you're a coffeeshop & they said we're
not a coffeeshop we're a hair salon so I said all right then,
a small haircut & a very attractive girl approached & said
right this way & she said would you like a complimentary cup
of coffee I said what the hell you told me there was no coffee
now you tell me there is coffee get your story straight bitch &
she said I'm Going To Have To Ask You To Leave so I jumped
up & down several times

## BILLY THE SNAKE

up ahead I spot a urinal but while I'm pissing in the
urinal a snake appears & starts talking to me & I begin to
suspect the snake is peeking which makes me a little
uncomfortable I am not attracted to snakes I do
not like snakes I say as much & the snake says The Floor
Is Nice To Pee On Too & I have to admit as I pee on the
floor the snake is right & by the time I wash my
hands the snake & I are good friends what should we
do now I don't even know your name & the snake said
My Name Is Billy What's Your Name then somehow
I guess the snake's mom called the police which as I
explained to the police was quite unnecessary Billy is
my friend I said & I guess I must have tried to play tag
with her but she was not a big fan of tag & the
police weren't either so much so they put me in jail can you
believe it anyway could you sign this form please

## ONCE UPON A TIME

let me tell you a Story I said to a very fat
man with a thick vest it's about a fat man just
like you & he said You Can't Smoke In Here & I said
but I'm not smoking anything can't you see I'm not
smoking anything & he said It Reeks Of Smoke In Here &
I said well let's you & I put that right by stealing all the
clocks & he said You Have To Put Those Clocks Back Where
They Came From & I said let me tell you a story & he
said It's Not Story Time It's Come With Me To The Dean's
Office Time so I threw a clock at him first one clock then
two clocks one clock two clock three clock four clock & my
hands disappeared which was very strange more fat men with
thick vests appeared & I asked them if they were on a bowling
team together & they say No well once upon a time

# THE JESTER KING


they poured ice in the urinals, just for fun
& their hands smelled of lemons & assholes

she stood apart from the others
& the streetlight shadows thrashed upon her face
the night the wind came down & tore the trees

this is a Pink Line train to 54th & Cermak
the homeless man rattles my change

she heard us whisper, never turned her head
to angel, tease & hipster sleaze, to all the things we said
she watched the glib hormonal fleas
sneak glances & imagine her in bed
& she sat down & asked us as our eyeballs fed
can someone get me a cigarette please?
of course, of course, anytime, I said

I stare as that man comes slouching back
it is a world of the sad & the strange

we watched her smile, shift & sneeze
she watched our cheeks turn red
I asked her is anything ever dead?
she laughed & uncrossed her naked knees
like the lake, how it won't ever freeze

I heard of a man who jumped onto the track
some ghost came slouching back

she nodded & said something & turned away
I watched her hair fly frantic in the breeze

the scholars, the dropouts, they're so very cool
they get their heads fed & they get their beds bread
at least for a little while

just then I realized I'd seen her before
on a stretcher they shoved through the ambulance door
yes that was me, she said, that happened last night
no one was there for me, everyone stared at me
guilt gripped us, & silence, then I spoke something soft
I spoke something cool & free & kind
& in her big blue eyes I saw her mind

polish your subways
jack off your cocks
their spindle's grown spitful
their doors have been locked

I brushed off her eyes a single dark strand
& thought of how it would be grand
to take her dancing in the sand

they clog up the gutters,
they clog up our eyes
we must loosen the shutters
we must swat all the flies

we left the ashtray garden
we left our silent friends

live up the world now
before it fills up with lies
fuck up the world now
it will get sterile with laughter

we walked along the water
we kicked our shoes off in the sand
we waded in the water
we kicked off our shirts in the sand

they walk fast,
they walk vacant
they creep & they crawl
these people could all be fake

we sat together in the sand
& got high
we talked about the universe
until the police came by

they walk slow
they're complacent
they sleep & they drawl
all of their teeth are at stake

I'm coursing through my veins
my blood cells & my eyes
I think I must be in my brain
she said with a sad ecstatic smile
I've left this world, this universe, this ceiling
& I won't be back for a while

they're calling your name
they're falling your game
walk fast, walk slow, walk perfect

is yoga played on football fields?
are bibles autographed by God?
I like you, boy, you're odd

I saw the mayor at my stop today
I stopped to hear what he had to say
the speech concerned the murders & rapes
they would be stopped without delay

what are you thinking? she said
we're not sinking, I said
well obviously, she said
exactly, I said
what do you mean? she said
just that, I said
can you explain? she said
I'll try, I said

I want to be the mayor
walk fast, walk slow, walk perfect

why does the man carry rocks in his pockets?
why are guitar heads hollow?
who walks through dreams with sand in their shoes?

who leads, & who needs, & who bleeds, & who follows?
who walks across the concrete plain?
who considers themselves a drop of rain?

things will change, say they
things never change, say they

do you get me? I said
if you kiss me, she said

I'll make changes, say they
I'll undo them, they say
it is a world of the sad & the strange, I say

so be it
so be us
so be everything that happens thus

I saw a man walking on a line
walk fast, walk slow, walk perfect

a giant monster was impossibly birthed out of human vagina
but don't stress it
don't stress us
it's bittersweet but life goes on
a wave of phoenix fire

swallowing up catastrophic minds vomit
swallowing up hitchhiking fingers
cold toes, cold minds
swallowing up our minds
& peace is rolling on the floor

I saw a man awaking sublime
walk fast, walk slow, walk perfect

why are our fingers that color?
why do we leave the heat for the hurricane?
why do we walk wet out of the water?
why do we sit silent in the sand?

what silver train took our minds off to jazz?
what janky joints jacked our minds out of jenga mildness?
what sad sleep tangled lonely sheets of cloth & introversion?
what bad strain of good medicine was vaporized
    in a one-bed room?
what swirl of sad smoke swam into our eyes?
what burned holes in our shorts?
whose face floated grinning in my dreams?

walk fast, walk slow, walk perfect
we had hope
look at all the flowers

lay in them
who lays in flowers?
stay back

watch the white in the rolling lake
watch the sun kids soak up cancer as they bake
watch the castles that they make
sit in the sand that the night winds rake
sneeze in the sand for God's sake
sip the cancer in the drags we take
watch the smoke in our long white wake
I told myself,
sit somewhere, count the raindrops, shade the stars
the fence bars, the cars come on from far away
sway the flowers in flowerpots
sway the kids in their flop hots

goodbye

you know what happens when the silence stops
you know the slipstream of the silver sun
you know she sits inside the sunny walls

walk fast, walk slow, walk perfect

I'll be there off the convoluted mind
I'll be there crawling when the shadows stop
I'll be there screaming in the smoky cell
I'll be there falling down the stairway stars

who is that walking down the sidewalk in the sun?
what bells ring? whose shadow falls upon me?
her shadow falls upon me

I saw a man shaking in slime
the sad things get you
the strange things stick
walk fast, walk slow, walk quick

# MOG

is it a game? does Mog have to play?

would prefer opium.

mortal Mog they captur'd

Mog's bones they crush'd

the wailing women they madly shush'd

prayerfully he wait here for the ax

even paid Mog his tithe & tax!

but did wrong

the song

for Oliver Cromwell

    let's fear Mog, they decided

     who cares if he's harmless, they confided

  fear car crash. fear not Mog. fear car crash.

       quietly quietly two by two

       the stars popp'd in the night, saw Mog from cell

       moon a no show, not feel so well

       Mog neither

  see how he say nothing in his own defense but mad garble?

   mad garble, bad garble, swish & spit a sad gargle/garble

     gargle gargoyle

       freak, they label'd him

send money, they cabl'd him

not a week later

hypocrites! assholes! jerks! meanies!

is Mog dead? is he a communist? t'was not Mog's part

is Mog a friend of England? surely! but they see not

his heart grocery basket cedar casket bury Mog with a girl


& a gasket

suggested Mog a punishment

less, eh, final

replied the magistrate: uh-uh. nope. sorry, son.

speedy Justice like instant coffee out-pouring came

one of its wings was both the same

(an old joke)

portending orphans—admonish'd England—handkerchief? bank
account? angel?

crystal balls/tea leaves/i ching

foster the roster/condemn the regicide/take a snot rag
with you wherever

checking accounts are sold/grow old get young again/be
bold eat dung, friend

demon! demon! cried Mog/angel, angel! cried the crowd

God save the Lord Protector! they said real loud

indigested petrol to doubt a gruff government's dogbone

Mog was hungry was all/swiped a candy or two/

hungry

was all/candy or two/hungry like me & hungry like you/
just a few

a schilling of petrol, madam/a schilling please/yes that's it,
thanks for these

reason/apology/central bank

season/biology/local skank

mouthfoaming… compos'd battle plans:

  deify most people

  supply the male enzyme to predominant money

  call Mog even less true

Mog soul appreciate in value, like real
estate

legacy & honor—fate!

Mog first second & third impression

in flag-fast & colorful succession

Mog interrupt the corrupt

  he stop a cop

he own a stone

  he eat meat

bailiff Mog a commotion felt; & so by the waist a broken girl
clean & neat & Mog lik'd her

  orgasms daily

  orgasms paid for

orgasms categorical

orgasms dusty

orgasms busty

but contributors to his decreasement pour'd

black evil spume on his name… she ador'd

& he scor'd

                              & she whor'd

& got bor'd

herbs with money, cypress, blue sky

                what & how kill Mog off, why?

song Mog sang

but was not enjoy'd

                no ice cubes

                no crushed ice

                no ice at all

                well if it isn't young Mog in a bathroom stall!

                bit of a reach, don't you think?

Mog a class A student

herbs with money, cypress, blue sky

                what? what? Mog, die?

herbs with money, cypress, blue sky

                how could be it the case?

quarrel'd Mog with democracy;

quarrel'd Mog with his chamber-pot;

quarrel'd Mog with the law

quarrel'd Mog with prophecy

quarrel'd Mog with the month of November

quarrel'd Mog with his dog

but quarrel'd Mog not with Connie. Connie was good. Connie
please Mog very much.

silver hats & silver queens

silver thoughts & silver Mog

the will that can

the understand

the fixable umbrella stand

Mog very lazy

Mog laughter ring out in Mog house

down Mog street Mog laughter waft

death trouble Mog very little

Mog took a correspondence course on it

Mog glad, really, to die tomorrow

a good run ran Mog

stopp'd short of outright treason Mog

but Oliver Cromwell in a straw hat?

Mog do miss Connie bad

Mog want to bend her over the radiator on a Sunday afternoon

Mog final wish for Connie to be spank'd

obliging lawyers

obliging gods

    overturned a table Mog; pleased the Lord Protector not

    jested Mog at Cromwell's coat

    very silly coat indeed

    would have looked better in a charcoal tweed

obliging majesties

obliging lords

obliging anyman Mog

Mog a peasant with a fat lapel

he do it wrong, every time, never no good

with hoe, shovel, rake, plow, scythe…no.

Mog go the way of Charles tomorrow.

all Mog want: his girl spank'd, & his story told!

Mog is tired & Mog is cold

              yes, yes, the Mog-tale…

              Mog's death-clothes gonna go on sale

Mog a dancer & met Connie that way

Mog buy Connie a hot dog

Mog one of the leading experts in fuck you

   when the storm it blew

   the windows off

   Mog very obvious a bad one

   Mog very obvious a mad one

Mog vulgar &

lugubrious

they call'd Mog bitch; cunt, Mog call'd back!

    fraudulent Mog they said

      evil Mog they claim'd

Mog a potty mouth


  THEY GONNA KILL MOG—behead him, yikes!

  they gonna poke him through with swords & pikes

  they gonna string him up as a warning for all

  Mog the brave & Mog the tall

  drag Mog on the floor & beat Mog on the wall

      Mog is fuck'd

## BROADCAST DOMINO PLAGUE

missionary ground epochs pave original aristocrats
sandaled fossils nakedly witness yellow eyes
rainbow bones knock scaffolding fear pictures

peaceful televisions condemn fanged posterchild
    choreography
brighter voices echo in the cathedrals of sainted popstars
shining armies ripple toward sinkholes assuming a causal
    relationship

singular fashions liquify accusations of logical connection
robotic runway microcosms strip away warning arrivals
steel hangars exemplify tribal justice flares

automatic vagina diagrams pluck roadside democracy
crossed world secrets plug carnivorous principles
horizon pall rears barred loyalties to the cornerstone

western dirges whip up oppressive smoke pledges
oceanic rhythms crash down on government addiction scripts
rising symphonies bombastically tearjerk face chains

frothy weapons epileptically broadcast domino plagues

drunken soldiers tower pathologically over gamed hospitals

breaking moons famously some distance from the pinball of
   bankruptcy

glass checkerboards pawned for gas money in the urgency
   typical of reinforcement

smiling masters enthrone fast beating swigs

modeling lemonade bloodlines with exhausted civil elixirs

barking at miniature needles divorced carelessly from youth

having climbed lesser problems dashingly in volleys of rebellion

despite the cuddles of unknown rails mirroring the reciprocated
   spank

not believing in arctic flowers' irrefutable irony spokes

rather napkins torn under tables into wasted temporary
   boomerangs

absorbing illegal conclusions with labyrinthine surf haircuts

# MERELY STRATEGIC BYLAWS

moments wander through a theater of decay
hourglass lions discourse about space
intersectional librarians meditate on an empty shelf
suicidal characters zoom toward a good workout routine
trinitarian junkies make a career out of waking up in the
    morning

colonial organs tangentially pulsate
indigenous gods receive sideways funerals
trailing off into merely strategic bylaws
serially slapping the wrists of dog food bureaucrats
so that pleuritic dancing erupts at experiential aquarian
    ceremonies

deriving the best course from lunar pole notch academies
fusing the arthritic dribble of tragedy with accomplishment's
    padded footrest
hairy murder victims make the Sunday papers
tasteful elevators indulge securely in shameful gossip
involving bitten off shirt buttons in bedroom claustrophobia
    tantrums

# THE LAST TO REALIZE WHAT DRIVES THEM

in a contrite posture the rabbi
signed off on a longer parade than was usual
having tripped acid with a locally renowned entomologist
who fell in love with the queen of the ants that live on his front walk

notwithstanding the extreme fog sixteen takes fast
fighting no urges the body flexes
war is attractive to thoughtless automatons
the last to realize what drives them

## LEWD WISDOM

plastic tasks implant lewd wisdom into solar taxation feints
illusory hoops ejaculate obsequious blonde epigrams onto a
    behaving tease

exclusive poker games curate anachronistically homogenous
    police cheerleaders
bouncing fireballs score high for damage done to suburban
    cog boxes

freed from cosmic numeral bongs smuggled into ancestral
    fluorescent basements
linking up with poorly traveled punk rockers under forgettable
    railroad bridges

# THE DESERT FOSSE

flanking mental corrosion with legibly scrawled lies
systemically criminal tentacular republics piss their inscrutable
    colors
piping into cages imperial speech freedoms to measurably
    deprive dreams
from anyone salty to swat the handsy agendas of oil barons

compostable anonymous guardian zeroes salute wide black
    margins
incorporated corpses bowed over bent recycling faceless enemy
    decimals
as needed string whatever dots hollow into strawman caves
offering in the desert fosse our wide eyed boys

# THIS BIBLIOGRAPHY

her island body millions calligraphically organize
into lipstick & shiny dragons in drywall scuffs
where muddy is the photographer with slimy notarized
    documents
& distilled the nudist who hopscotches into safe clouds

so toss me the aux cord & don't swerve into bank shadows
unless you want to shark the gospel of its hypnotic justified
    columns
revisited symbiotically such gazebos as my index finger
yodeling quietly under the arches of this bibliography

## BUSINESS FANTASIES

vain fancy chasms purely merging with blurred packages
weathering velvety input & showered with guidelines, a pink
    part
so gangsterish wares won't qualify her specific embarrassments
& glass figurines shall not be blown, it would encircle & bang
    bang
business fantasies we will sweep off like so many love letters
such that six oblong prostitutes lift the pall off my coffin

# AJAR BUT MARRIAGEABLE GIRLS

critically parroting gravelly darkness, the finite radio
annotates the unified undergrowth & in small mirrors eyes
chalk up nomance to spiraling messages in green bottles &
    economy
lax teachably cradling symptomatic jealousies & shine
    rhythmic vaults
ajar but marriageable girls mobilize their tooth genies &
    dance mysteriously
canned ceremonial virginities by the pound & sip cloudy
    exotic tablatures

## PRODIGAL DENOMINATORS

risky heights & penitentially dribbles an anxious bloomer
perhaps rescuing dolled soda jerks from Kansas verticals
doctrinally sealing pharaoh tombs with hollow chronological
    paradigms
so pontifical gaffes compose par slender & circumscribe
    discipleship

gabardine haters & take trains to the first resort; rapid the
    followed fox
sailing downvotes into pornographic rabbit holes & prophesy
    mass loneliness
hot her coolness; I understand lost prescient statistical outliers
voicing unfashionable allegiance to prodigal denominators

## OBSESSIVE SANDCASTLES

funky victories harden into the whole world
steep goalposts immovably subjected to sweeping theories

grammatical skyscrapers presently demolished at bestial games
buttoned-up lucid dreams wash away obsessive sandcastles

## THE USUAL VOWS

frail educations piously utter salt-beloved goners
sugaring diagrams knelt before silent iron lattice
inappropriately correlating gold with coughed-out wholesale roses
moving to weld futures, regurgitate the usual vows

# VIGOROUS HOMOSEXUAL ENDORSEMENTS

giddily excising death kiosks from tenaciously analyzed
    metropicide
daddy's taking off his pants; doctors are exchanging
    vigorous homosexual endorsements

the rotund fisherman can't quite hear what the gesticulating
    physicist is saying to the small barber
normally, the bishop wouldn't perform this particular
    motion with his right hand, but it is indeed a
    time of widespread socio-coronary malaise

always the altar boy snuffs out the light of Christ, not
    the other way around, OK?— meanwhile, at the
    strip clubbiest of strip clubs,  I am as difficult as a whetstone,
    mmhm, & it's very bad
& only once shall the urchin manage to satiate the ghost of the
    maternal dead wonderful

## SWINDLED MOON SYLLABLES

spidering truths enfather swindled moon syllables
tweaking presidents divorcing grift & grafting to nations bad
   languages

tweezer executrix: I desire colored pencils & want nothing of
   criminate villainy strobes
to which the washing machine mascot: let's not segregate the
   architecture of this pointy grayscale..

such as it is, the other appliances chorally: eat shit, poverse
   beams of unicorn city!
& now everybody can sing the diapering mathematics of
   alchemized myth spliffers

# A GARDEN VARIETY BACKHOE

spelling daily pavement councils, her kinked-out
    summerhouse pigtails
add up to offseason sky congressionals & she is a garden
    variety backhoe
or, sum up thine sinfinities toward one big snakeskin condom
in response to all this talk of clitoral figuration & goons are
    basking in the dune-pile

## AND IT'S ALL VERY VIOLENT AND PEACEFUL

remote midnights cobble brackish distance
controlled arctic hypotheses slake far-off isms
financially South American hierophants elope with burnt
    crackers & a book of Mark Fisher essays
& central hombres substantiate lost buoyant Mossad honeys

I must say that asymmetrical thrusting will not cause the
    princess to arrive at the forbidden happy-castle
so naturally—a pull here & a push there—she
gasping in a yes YES paroxysm accepts your garrison of little
    swimmers
& it's all very violent & peaceful

# THE EX-BARISTA

liably occupied sunset fables advertise constant whooshing
   sounds
preventable Israels blush at convenient speeches & I never
   speed

geologic liberties flash cashiers, who say nothing; don't you
   want some?
jogged & wrongly has the flesh been serviceably
   merchandised… at least look at them!

endangering objective morality with explicit legalese & nosy
   preferred customers
having already fired the only decent barista for breaching
   the secret dress code

## PSYCHIATRY

buried haunts assemble fostered afflictions
monochromatic libraries ascribe to the children diagnoses
darkly shelving their names in oversize cabinets
& in the morning new intake forms receive unsuitable
    paragraphs

## DIAMONDS, FIREMEN & NEOCONS

contemplative clutches joy filter indolent spleens heroically
masked assailants pop the inner monologues of laconic
    Parisian firefighters

scary means align themselves with scary ends; on small stages
    strut exotic princes
neocon airplanes banner neocon Halliburtons & children
    labor in Congo diamond mines

# THE CONSTANT SPECTER OF PARLIAMENT

unclaimed stars cautiously greet published mailmen
teary-eyed backup dancers reverentially salute a phalanx
    of lawyers
reducing to photography the ancient practice of
    raising one's glass to award-winning documentary
    filmmakers in all seriousness

whiskey barrels topple down, tragically killing multiple
    Russian tourists & you can watch the whole fiasco on
    the internet
grizzled has-beens refrain from purchasing airline
    tickets, fearing the curious inquiries of stray bloggers
obese monarchs hum a tune here & there as a way of
    escaping the constant specter of parliament

glacial legislative debates rhythmically erupt with angry
    exhortations to get real, which are always ignored
vestigial rules occasionally rear their mummified heads
    to gobble up the hours
& emergency breaches of protocol routinely trip up
    attention-seeking orators

# THE FUMES OF VOLITION

disdainful platforms infest market-priced hungover
    desecrators
swooping senators gnaw at scarce photophobic watering cans

fumes of volition cast doubt-shade on museum-quality torture
    implements
laughing uncontrollably the jury can't get past the dental
    anecdote

## BURLAP DISGUISES

war's white bathtub exponentially flunks the age
chalice abstractions curb vegan victims of dimmer switches
blind galleries flush blockbuster handshakes romantically
neglected restaurants approve serpentine opaque sculptures

backseat craftsmen legislate ironically profitable heroes
restrained organic monuments dismantle burlap disguises
mentally virginal & asserting predictability recruits allow to
    become distorted
the venomous gynecological geometries that alarm volunteerist
    spin doctors

scaly & a concave manuscript awakens the earliest goldsmiths
difficult to grasp railroads endure bruising totals luxuriously
recreational linearities grandly gaslight traumatized
    psychotherapists
high altitude futures tally nostalgic watchwords chorally

inebriated architects box up sepia flags as one
guilted hatchet men redeem enemy anthems at karaoke
conscious telephones altruistically bump the popular confessions
shampooed dualist pastry chefs inhale confidential denominators

pared-down philosophers swish unappetizing speciesist
    storefronts
minimalist jewelers rudely command Darwinian soccer teams
painters interrogate proletarian foot soldiers at prosaic getaways
bragging royal bloodlines well-organized spokesmen close
    curtains

catalog narcotics weave Euclidean podiums climactically
clocking unweatherable sales pitches at well-attended EDM
    festivals
it's a race; morally fluid excretions punctuate the summer
    solstice
Masonic relics drown extraneous temporary landmarks

## STRATEGICALLY IRRELEVANT MUTILATION

tomorrow's women maze lectured-on pirated paragraphs
reflecting unwritten screams & dreaming of power the scholar
parries perforated gifts to science with champagne electric
    darkness
& in reply the abyss fronts the necessary seeds of behavior

canonical adversaries dime the feast of the weed-eager
    epistolarian
& in the trenches noble flutterings of sacrifice virally take root
but in the bunkers a sinister musculature sheds the natural
    vestments
causing strategically irrelevant mutilation

## THIS PILE OF MISDIRECTED AGGRESSIONS


sloping gracefully into convicted business impossible
    graduates
lob at sincere bridges compartmentalized cosmic rituals
reluctantly facing the salutary death jackets, not to be
    confused with the constellations of instinct


alerted to possible alien proclamations blinking cryptically
    toward this pile of misdirected aggressions
vigilant defenders of contradictory mission statements dial
    their doublespeaking nominal commander
who then drowsily assembles the applicable players: The Liar,
    The Slacker, The Scientist, The Yes Man


& they all agreed: the regime as we know it hangs from the
    string of their preempting that which would capsize
    continents & infect the living
with terror & chaos & killing & all manner of barbarism &
    cutting in line
so with bad faces they argued & refuted & fought & disputed,
    interrupting counterpoints with sophomoric ad hominem &
    shouting down bad ideas with good ideas, until all but one
    lost their voices…

## THE CONCLUDING REMARKS OF GOD

shadowing assuaged weighty comrade fleecings oozed-on
    planetary throngs anonymize operative shibboleths
ditched bandages hook the friendly survivalists who loiter in
    the vestibules of the new masjid which already has a
    reputation for fiery khutbahs
cowboy surgeons convert a stray railroad spike to the only
    legitimate orbital postulate which states in the fashion of
    shahadah the concluding remarks of God

## DELUGE THIRTEEN

Here—ye have heard & seen—now this thirteenth
deluge. Taste it!
                    Aren't you afraid of
Jerusalem? Pour forth, & passionately! Will the woman whose

        Hollywood

        bright lights

        & howling

        says something
                    About the invisible soul
                    About this country
                    About your daughter's groceries
[dead, dead,]    About the dead  the dead   the dead  the dead—
how dead the dead Dead
                              open wide? Will she
                    be incapable of change? Will she
            be the only one in touch with me? Will she
            invent the universe? No.

                                        Will she

        invent some monstr
        ous urge to continu

e vindicating such
magic as salvation?????

                    That's
                    a big
                    no-no. We don't ask that around
here.

## WHAT IF THE DEVIL IS SORRY

summer. the wicked boys
  graffiti an appea
  l to the pope  on
  the locked  doub
  le doors of a  riv
  al church down t
  he road

## THE REPUBLIC

1
the Republic is frustrated with itself
things used to be very nice
now things are bad
what happened?

2
the Republic is having a bad hair day
maybe the Republic should have slept
in their own bed for once
the Republic is such a slut

3
the Republic sometimes doesn't even
think it's even a Republic
the Republic can be
kind of hard on itself

4
it wasn't always like this
kingdoms used to turn their heads
when the Republic would pass them
on the street

5

one time the Republic took a liking

to this kingdom

an older kingdom

with a big military

## CHERYL IS A GRAY-HAIRED WHITE WOMAN

Cheryl is a gray-haired white woman.
She has a pet cockroach.
The theatre has really gone downhill.
Cheryl is a gray-haired white woman.

Cheryl is a gray-haired white woman.
Cheryl is a gray-haired white woman.
She thought about getting a dog, but didn't.
We're lucky we have Jesus.

Sooner or later Cheryl is gonna die.
She's not in a rush, though.
Cheryl is a gray-haired white woman.
Cheryl is a gray-haired white woman.

Cheryl is a gray-haired white woman.

## LUCKY PERSON

My boss is smoking a cigar in a golden Chevy parked outside a
    McDonald's.
An eagle shits on his windshield & she shouts a racial slur at
    the eagle.
A McDonald's employee takes off his pants so that he can
    enjoy a slurpee.

I consider myself a lucky person.

## LIVING CONDITIONS

The dolls are missing arms. The revolution better hurry up.

Hart L'Ecuyer was born in the South. He only has one eye. As a rule he prefers the company of women. He has been arrested three times. He has been sent to the psych ward twice. He prefers mountains to beaches, as much as he loves beaches.

This project was made possible, in part, by generous support from the Osage Arts Community.

Osage Arts Community provides temporary time, space and support for the creation of new artistic works in a retreat format, serving creative people of all kinds — visual artists, composers, poets, fiction and nonfiction writers. Located on a 152-acre farm in an isolated rural mountainside setting in Central Missouri and bordered by ¾ of a mile of the Gasconade River, OAC provides residencies to those working alone, as well as welcoming collaborative teams, offering living space and workspace in a country environment to emerging and mid-career artists. For more information, visit us at www.osageac.org

Osage Arts Community